THE ILLUSTRATED ENCYCLOPEDIA
of STEAM WORDS

An A-Z of 100 Terms Kids NEED to Know!

Racehorse for Young Readers books may be purchased in bulk at special discounts for sales promotions, corporate gifts, fund-raising or education purposes. Special editions can also be created to specifications. For details, contact the Special Sales Department at Skyhorse Publishing, 307 West 36th Street, 11th Floor, New York, NY 10018 or info@skyhorsepublishing.com.

Racehorse for Young Readers is a pending trademark of Skyhorse Publishing, Inc.®, a Delaware corporation.

Visit our website at skyhorsepublishing.com

10 9 8 7 6 5 4 3 2 1

Library of Congress Cataloging-in-Publication Data is available on file.

Art director: Vicky Barker
Publisher: Sam Hutchinson

Printed in China by WKT Co. Ltd. on FSC-certified paper.

ISBN
978-1-63158-681-1

THE ILLUSTRATED ENCYCLOPEDIA

of STEAM WORDS

An A-Z of **100** Terms Kids NEED to Know!

Written by **JENNY JACOBY**   Illustrated by **VICKY BARKER**

FOR YOUNG READERS

CONTENTS

HOW TO USE THIS BOOK

This encyclopedia explains one hundred words from the worlds of science, technology, engineering, art, and mathematics (known all together as STEAM). Each word has its own page, where you'll learn what the word means, along with some amazing facts, all made easy to understand with simple, charming illustrations.

The pages come in alphabetical order, from **A**daptation to **Z**oology. It's fun to pick up the book at a random page and see what you find, but if you want to look up a particular word, check the listings on the **Contents** page (see pages 4 and 5).

As each key word is explained, lots more STEAM words related to the idea are introduced. These extra words are highlighted in bold in the text, and a short definition of each can be found in the **Index** at the back, which doubles up as a glossary.

The world of STEAM is full of exciting words and ideas that you might not have come across before. There are many more than one hundred! If you hear about an idea you would like to know more about but it isn't one of the main topics listed on the **Contents** page, try looking it up in the **Index**.

HAPPY READING!

WHAT IS STEAM?

STEAM stands for "science, technology, engineering, art, and mathematics." These areas are closely linked, and each one supports the others and also inspires ideas in the others.

SCIENCE is studying the natural world by observing it, and then testing out ideas about how it works to get an even deeper understanding—from things smaller than an atom to bigger than Jupiter.

TECHNOLOGY and **ENGINEERING** both use the knowledge of the world that science discovers to create tools and machines that help us live our lives better and solve problems in the world.

Communicating ideas is vital in all STEAM subjects.

ART uses creative thought to inspire ideas and to express those ideas. Artists use technology to create art and artists also inspire new technology and engineering ideas.

MATHEMATICS uses numbers and techniques to uncover some of the rules of the natural world. Math also supports all the STEAM subjects to make sure their work is accurate.

ADAPTATION

Adaptation is a word used in biology to describe how living things have **evolved** so that they can live successfully in their environment.

Charles Darwin came up with his theory of evolution when he noticed that each different **species** of finch living on a different **Galapagos island** had a slightly different beak shape that was perfectly adapted to suit the food available to it on its island.

The finches that eat insects have the thinnest beaks, while the finch that crushes hard seeds has a large, stout beak. The finch that feeds on seeds from cacti has a long, pointed beak.

Too well adapted?

The **dodo** was a bird that lived on Mauritius. It adapted to its environment by losing the ability to fly—it didn't need to fly because there was plenty of good food for it to eat and no **predators** to threaten it. That was until European sailors turned up on the island—and hunted the dodo to **extinction** as it was so easy to capture.

AI

AI stands for "artificial intelligence" and it is a technology that tries to make computers learn and think like humans.

Computers are great at doing what they are instructed to do but with AI, computers can think for themselves.

They do this by taking in information (**input**) and making a decision on how to react. The input could be **data** provided by humans or other computers, or readings from the outside world, such as **temperature**, the number of cars on the road or pollution levels.

AI is so useful because computers can process a lot more information than humans alone can. AI can find patterns that a human might not have noticed, and suggest issues for humans to think about, such as looking at weather patterns to predict a storm coming.

What AI can't do

There are some things AI cannot do, such as imagining new ideas, or transferring the lessons learned in one subject to another one. Making these sorts of inventive connections is left to humans—that's the fun part!

SUNDAY   MONDAY   TUESDAY

9

ALGORITHM

An algorithm is an idea taken from mathematics and it means a step-by-step way of solving a problem. The steps need to be very clear and they must be followed exactly. At some point, the steps end and give a final result.

Computer **programs** need algorithms to do certain tasks but an algorithm can also describe something **analogue**, which means not computer-based, such as tidying your room. The algorithm needs to have an **input**, a **process** and an **output**. The steps are different for each problem.

Ancient algorithms!

Algorithms are famous for being part of very successful online search engines or online shopping platforms. But over 2,000 years ago, in the year 300 BCE, the ancient Greek mathematician Euclid wrote one to solve a mathematical problem. The term "algorithm" was first used by a Muslim mathematician in the ninth century.

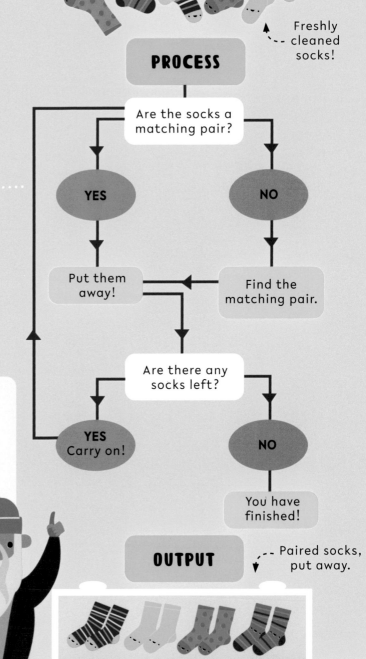

INPUT

Freshly cleaned socks!

PROCESS

Are the socks a matching pair?

YES — NO

Put them away! — Find the matching pair.

Are there any socks left?

YES Carry on! — NO

You have finished!

OUTPUT — Paired socks, put away.

ALTERNATING CURRENT

Alternating current is the way electricity powers our household electrical items.

Electricity flows around a **circuit** in a "current."

Electricity works because the **electrons** (tiny parts of an **atom**) in the metal wires flow from the negative side of the battery to the positive side. This is called **direct current**, because the electricity flows in one direction, and is used in small battery-powered items.

CURRENT

WIRE

LIGHT

BATTERY

SWITCH

Household items that are plugged into the mains supply use alternating current. This is because alternating current is more efficient for sending high **voltage** electricity across the country from power stations to homes.

Good vibrations

Alternating current is when the electrons don't flow around the circuit in one direction but repeatedly switch directions so that they vibrate. This means the power very quickly changes from on to off and back again—this happens so quickly that we don't notice.

ANATOMY

Anatomy is the part of biology to do with studying the body—how it looks and how all the pieces fit and work together.

To study the internal anatomy of an animal or plant, a scientist carefully cuts it open and examines the parts found inside. This is called **dissection**. They might photograph or draw what they see, and compare its size, looks and condition to other examples.

Today, we can use machines to look inside people's bodies safely and painlessly while they are alive, using an **MRI scanner**.

We can even see the anatomy of unborn babies using **ultrasound** scanners to check that their bodies are growing well. (See page 89.)

Ancient anatomy

Five hundred years ago, **Leonardo da Vinci** studied anatomy by looking at bodies in hospitals and carefully observing and drawing them. By learning about anatomy, he understood how muscles work, and this understanding helped inspire some of his inventions.

ATOMS

Atoms are the building blocks of our entire universe. They combine in different ways to make everything, from solid objects to liquids and gases, but on their own they are very small and scientists need a special type of microscope to see them.

There are three main parts of an atom:

protons, **neutrons**, and **electrons**.

The protons and the neutrons make up the center of the atom and together they are called the **nucleus**. The electrons surround the nucleus.

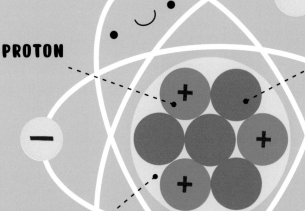

PROTON

NEUTRON

NUCLEUS

ELECTRON

An atom of the gas called neon contains ten protons, ten neutrons, and ten electrons. Every atom with ten protons is a neon atom since it is the number of protons that defines an atom.

Super-powered machinery!

Atoms are very small! It would take roughly fifty million atoms to measure one centimeter. Scientists use a transmission electron microscope (TEM) to see them. The TEM fires a beam of electrons to create an image that the human eye can see.

BAROMETER

A **barometer** is a tool for measuring the **air pressure**, which helps in **meteorology**. There are a few different types of barometer but they all tell us how much the air around us weighs.

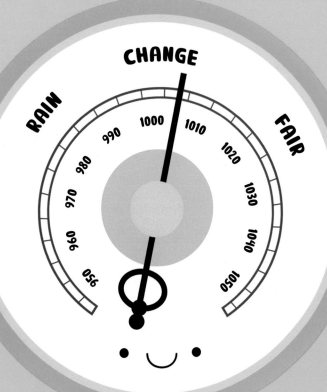

RAIN

CHANGE

FAIR

950 960 970 980 990 1000 1010 1020 1030 1040 1050

Although air feels light it is made up of **molecules** of various gases, which are always moving about. Sometimes there are more—when the air pressure is high. Other times there are fewer—when the air pressure is low.

High air pressure usually means the weather will be fair and dry but in low pressure rain, snow, or hail is likely.

How high?

Barometers can also be used to measure **altitude**. The higher the altitude the lower the air pressure, while the closer you are to sea level the higher the pressure because there is more air above you.

BIG BANG

The big bang is the start of the universe. Before it there was nothing, and ever since the big bang the universe has been expanding. It happened over a very short time—a matter of seconds!

The universe started very small and quickly expanded in size. It was hot and dense at the beginning, and this is when all **matter** particles were formed, called **quarks**.

After millions of years, the universe developed **light**, stars, galaxies, **Earth**, and each of us—all made from the atoms generated in the big bang.

The bigger the universe grew, the cooler it got. The tiny quark particles grouped together to form **atoms**, starting with **hydrogen**.

BIG BANG

H

What we don't know

We don't know what happened the moment before the big bang. We don't know if it was the first beginning of the first universe, or if other universes had existed before ours. We don't know why it occurred or what started it.

BIOLUMINESCENCE

Bioluminescence is a special glow given off by some plants and animals. It can be caused by **bacteria** in the animal, or by the animal itself.

There are bioluminescent animals of all different kinds living on land and in the sea. They produce light for different reasons.

About three-quarters of deep-sea animals produce light, for defense or warning, but the bioluminescent creatures people most often see at sea are the **plankton** that live near the surface and glow at night as the sea froths.

On land, fireflies and glow-worms can be seen on summer evenings as they glow to try to attract a **mate**.

Alluring

The deep-sea anglerfish has a glowing lure called an esca that dangles from its head to attract prey towards it. The esca glows because of bacteria that live on it in **symbiosis**.

BROWNIAN MOTION

Brownian motion is the name for the way particles move randomly in gases and liquids. It is also known as **pedesis**, which comes from the Greek word for "leaping."

The easiest way to see Brownian motion is watching dust motes floating in the sunlight.

VISIBLE

INVISIBLE

They don't move in any regular, planned way, like a fly might, but seem to bob about from one place to another, never staying still.

This happens because all the particles in the air (and in liquids) are constantly moving and knocking into each other. The dust particles are only the visible part of air, which is full of moving particles.

Robert Brown

Brownian motion takes its name from Robert Brown, the scientist who first observed this random movement when he looked at **pollen** grains moving in water under a microscope, in 1827. He observed the motion but couldn't explain it—that took until 1905 when **Albert Einstein** came up with an explanation.

17

BUNSEN BURNER

A Bunsen burner is a piece of equipment used in a science **laboratory** (lab). It burns gas to give a single flame that is easy to control, and is used to heat, sterilize or burn chemicals in **experiments**.

AIR HOLE CLOSED

AIR HOLE OPEN

The gas flows through a rubber pipe into the burner. The flame burns at the top when the gas is lit by a match or lighter. A valve on the base controls how much gas flows through, and how much air mixes in with the gas. By varying the gas and air mixture, the burner can produce different types of flame.

With no air added a "safety flame" burns long and yellow so it's visible. With the air hole open, the flame burns hotter and blue, almost invisible.

Robert Bunsen

German scientist Robert Bunsen invented the equipment in the 1850s when he helped design his new laboratory at the University of Heidelberg, Germany. Heidelberg was beginning to use gas lighting on streetlamps so the university was able to bring gas pipes to the lab. Today they are used in labs around the world.

CHLOROPHYLL

Chlorophyll is a chemical that plants use to turn sunlight into food, in the process called **photosynthesis**. It's what gives plants their green color.

Chlorophyll's important job sustains all life on the planet: it is a **photoreceptor**, which means it traps sunlight.

It uses the power of sunlight to create **sugar** from air and **water**. The plant uses that sugar for its own food, but as we—and lots of other animals—eat plants, we also get our **energy** indirectly from the Sun.

Plants that grow with little or no light are weaker and paler in color because with less light there is less chlorophyll.

Color change

New leaves in spring are pale green; in summer they turn darker and in autumn many leaves change to yellow, orange or red as the chlorophyll breaks down, to be reabsorbed by the tree for next spring. The autumn colors are suited to trap the lower levels of autumn sunlight.

CHROMOSOME

A **chromosome** is a pair of long strands of the molecule **DNA**, found in the **nucleus** of every **cell** in the body (apart from red blood cells). DNA contains genetic material (**genes**) which are the **code** needed to build everything in your body.

CHROMOSOME

DOUBLE HELIX

Each chromosome is made of a double strand of DNA, twisted into a double helix.

When the cell wants to create a **protein** (a building block for the body), the chromosome opens up so the code on one of the strands can be 'read', which is called **transcription**.

DNA

Another part of the cell called a **ribosome** uses the code to build the protein.

Different numbers

Humans have 23 pairs of chromosomes inside their cells but other animals and plants have different numbers. One chromosome comes from a female and one from a male, making each individual a half-half mix of each biological parent. This means there are two options for each chromosome but usually only one of each pair is "expressed," like with eye color.

1	2	3		4	5
6	7	8	9	10	11	12
13	14	15		16	17	18
19	20		21	22		X	Y

COALESCENCE

Coalescence means to come together, and in **physics** and chemistry it describes when two or more particles come together to form one new whole.

Many types of particles can coalesce at different scales, from tiny to big.

In **meteorology**, water droplets coalesce in a cloud until they are big enough to fall as rain—and you might see raindrops coalesce as they run down a window.

In **astrophysics**, **matter** might coalesce to create a new star.

Attraction

When water droplets come close and make the slightest contact, they coalesce immediately—they seem to pull at each other. Once they have coalesced, the new, bigger droplet is called a "daughter" droplet.

COGNITION

Cognition means thinking, and how we **process** the information that comes into our brains from all that we experience.

Lots of different things make up our thinking processes, which together influence our cognition. They are the **inputs** coming into our minds, what our brains do with those inputs, and how we express our thoughts.

The inputs include how we perceive or sense the world, while thinking is influenced by how much attention we pay, how much we already know, our memories, how we reason, make decisions and solve problems.

Other minds

Other animals think differently from us and sometimes the best way to understand our own cognition is to compare it to others'. By teaching sign language to a gorilla, scientists learned that gorillas are great communicators, can learn language like a human child and can express many of the same emotions we feel.

COPROLITE

Coprolite is the science word for fossilized **feces**. Feces is the science word for poo!

Coprolites are very useful to **paleontologists** because looking at faeces can tell them a lot about what an animal ate—whether it ate plants or meat, and what sort of meat.

Fossils of an animal's body can give a lot of clues to the animal's life, but its coprolites can tell us about its behavior—which is otherwise very hard to know for an **extinct** animal.

Mary Anning

Mary Anning was a fossil hunter from Lyme Regis, England, in the early 1800s, who discovered stones in the abdomen of ichthyosaur fossils. She looked inside coprolites and found fossils of fish scales and bone. William Buckland, a geologist of the time, realized that they were looking at fossilized feces and named them coprolites.

DATA

Data is information that has been collected through research. Data provides the facts that lots of other work is based on. It can help researchers choose what to explore next, and help campaigners persuade people to make improvements. Working with data is called **statistics**.

When scientists want to investigate an idea, the first thing they must do is gather information, called data. There are several ways to collect data, such as observing, counting, performing **tests**, asking questions—and it all has to be noted down.

Data can be presented in tables and in graphs and charts. Then it is easier to understand the subject and notice anything unusual, interesting or that could be improved.

Florence Nightingale

Famous for her nursing, Florence Nightingale was especially effective because she collected data that nobody at the military hospital had before. She counted the number of soldiers dying, their cause of death, and deaths per month. Her charts showed that a big cause of death was the unclean conditions in the hospital.

DECIDUOUS

Deciduous trees lose their leaves once a year, in winter, growing new ones again in spring.

Deciduous forests are found in parts of the world that have four clear seasons each year.

In winter, deciduous trees have no leaves as protection against the cold and to avoid losing water.

In spring, new, light green leaves unfurl from buds.

In summer, leaves turn darker green thanks to their **chlorophyll** turning the Sun's energy into food for the tree.

In autumn, leaves turn yellow, orange or red, then brown as the tree shuts off the leaves, leaving them to die and fall off.

Evergreen

In places where winters are long and cold, with a lot of rain or snow, trees are evergreen, meaning they keep their green leaves all year long. Pine, spruce, and fir trees have thin, waxy needles rather than leaves, which are tough enough to survive long winters and strong winds, and don't lose water.

DIFFRACTION

Diffraction is what happens to **waves** as they pass through an opening. There are many different types of wave, including **sound** and light, but they behave in the same way, spreading out after they pass through the gap.

If the waves meet an obstacle with an opening they will travel through the gap. On the other side, the waves curve outwards, called diffraction.

WAVELENGTH
(SHOWN AS THE SPACE BETWEEN THE LINES)

If the opening is about as wide as the **wavelength**, the waves spread around the corners of the opening, diffracting more strongly. If the opening is wider than the wave's wavelength then the diffraction effect is weaker.

BLOCKED LINE OF SIGHT

HI

DOORWAY

Listening at doors

Because sound waves have a wavelength of about the width of a door, you can stand next to an open doorway and clearly hear a conversation behind the wall, even if you can't see who is talking. The trick works less well at a wider opening because the gap is wider than the wavelength, so the waves diffract less.

DNA

DNA is a **molecule** that contains the genetic material all living things need to grow and **reproduce**.

DNA's long strands are made up of a 'backbone' of a **sugar** and attached at even intervals along the backbone are one of four other chemicals:

adenine
guanine
cytosine
thymine

These chemicals like to pair with one particular other chemical, and this pairing causes the DNA strands to double up with another strand.

ADENINE pairs with **THYMINE**

GUANINE pairs with **CYTOSINE**

What's in a name?

DNA stands for "**d**eoxyribo**n**ucleic **a**cid." Deoxyribose is the name of the sugar that forms the backbone of the strand, and it is a nucleic **acid** because it is an acid found in the **nucleus** of **cells**.

27

DYNAMITE

Dynamite is an explosive that was invented in the 1860s by Alfred Nobel. It was the safest yet most powerful explosive available and was used for blasting rock, to clear space for construction and exploration—which was happening all over the world in the nineteenth century.

DETONATOR

EXPLOSIVE

FUSE

PROTECTIVE COATING

Before dynamite, **nitroglycerin** was the most powerful explosive, but it was too dangerous to use as it could be set off unexpectedly.

Alfred invented dynamite by mixing nitroglycerin with a white powder called **kieselgur** that made it safe until detonated, and it could be shaped into rods.

Dynamite became so popular that Alfred made a fortune, and it's still used today in mining, construction and demolition.

Nobel Prize

Towards the end of his life, Nobel worried about his legacy, and wanted to use his fortune for peace. So, he set up the Nobel Foundation, which awards Nobel Prizes each year for the most exceptional work in the fields of chemistry, literature, peace activism, physics and physiology or medicine.

ALFR-NOBEL

NAT-MDCCC XXXIII OB MDCCC XCVI

DYNAMO

A dynamo is a machine for turning movement into electricity. It is a simple electricity generator and was one of the first inventions for producing electrical current.

Dynamos produce electricity by using motion energy to turn a magnet inside a coil of copper wire.

The laws of **electromagnetism** (see page 32) mean this action starts electricity flowing through the wire.

MAGNET CASE

AXLE

AXLE

COIL OF COPPER WIRE

The motion energy can come from almost anywhere—wind, water, steam, or muscle power! The power a dynamo creates depends on the power going in (the speed the magnet turns at) and the amount of copper wire used (how many times it has been wound around its iron core).

MAGNET

COIL OF WIRE

WIRES GOING TO LAMP

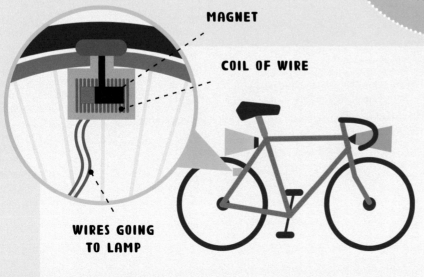

Bicycle light

Dynamo lights on bicycles work by using the spinning bicycle wheel to turn a magnet inside a copper wire. The electricity produced goes to the bicycle lamp so that the light goes on while the wheels are turning.

ECHOLOCATION

Echolocation is a way of finding things through listening to the echoes of sounds. The animal sends out bursts of sound and listens to how long the echoes take to return to learn where things are. It is "seeing" with sound.

Lots of different kinds of animals use echolocation.

BAT CALL

ECHO

Bats use it because they fly and hunt at night and it is their version of night **vision**. Some marine **mammals** like dolphins and porpoises use it to find friends and prey far away from them in the murky sea.

In echolocation, animals can adjust how far or how wide they send their sounds depending on where they are "looking."

Human echolocation

Some people can teach themselves echolocation to find their way around without the use of their eyes. It's a skill humans have to train themselves to do, and people develop their own methods, such as tapping a cane or making clicking noises with their mouth.

CLICK

ECOSYSTEM

An **ecosystem** is an idea from biology describing how all of the **organisms** (plants, animals and **bacteria**) living in a community interact with each other and with their physical environment.

In an ecosystem, everything is dependent on everything else.

The non-living parts influence what types of plant, animal and bacteria can live there. That includes the climate (the **temperature** and how much it rains), the soil and available water.

When the ecosystem is in balance, each part helps give life to the other parts.

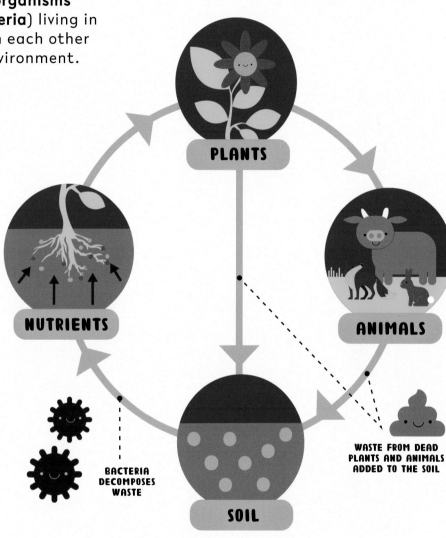

PLANTS

NUTRIENTS

ANIMALS

BACTERIA DECOMPOSES WASTE

WASTE FROM DEAD PLANTS AND ANIMALS ADDED TO THE SOIL

SOIL

A healthy ecosystem

Changing one element of an ecosystem will impact everything else. Animals get their **nutrients** by eating the plants growing there, and the animals return nutrients to the soil with their waste. Also, when plants and animals die, bacteria, and insects break them down into nutrients that help more plants to grow.

31

ELECTROMAGNETISM

Electromagnetism is the way magnets and electrical current interact. It is a law of nature that magnets and electricity influence each other: electricity flowing creates a magnetic field around the wire, and a magnet turning around copper wire creates electrical current.

In 1831 Michael Faraday discovered that passing a magnet through a coil of wire starts electricity flowing through the wire.

Today most electricity is made in the same way. Giant turbines in power stations turn movement into electricity.

Steam, wind or water spin turbine blades that spin a coil of copper wire within a magnet case. Electricity then flows through the wire and out into the power grid, where it travels to homes and buildings.

BAR MAGNET

INSULATION

COPPER WIRE

Electromagnets

When current runs through a copper wire that has been wrapped around iron, it creates an electromagnet—a magnet that can be turned off and on. This is useful in places such as scrapyards, where electromagnets can attract metal objects, move them and then release them at the flick of a switch.

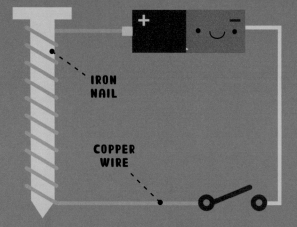

IRON NAIL

COPPER WIRE

EVAPORATE

Evaporation is when a liquid turns into a gas. You might notice this when a puddle—made of liquid water—gradually disappears on a dry day. This is because the water evaporates into **water vapor** in the air.

Evaporation is happening all the time, as water from rivers, ponds and even food and drink evaporates into the air.

The amount of water vapor in the air changes all the time and there is a limit to how much the air can carry. The less water vapor in the air, the easier it is for water to evaporate because the air has "space" for more.

The amount of water in the air is called the **humidity**.

Misty mornings

Evaporation is often invisible—you won't see it happening apart from the liquid disappearing. But on cold mornings you might notice a mist over fields as dew (water) on the grass evaporates, and then condenses again in the cold air. **Condensation** is the opposite of evaporation, where water vapor becomes liquid again.

FERTILIZER

Fertilizer is food for plants to help them grow. It contains the **nutrients** plants need and can be **organic** or **synthetic**. Plants absorb the nutrients through their roots in the soil.

Waste (poo and pee) from animals contains nutrients the body doesn't need. It acts as an organic fertilizer when it lands on the soil and the nutrients are absorbed back into the ground.

Compost is made from plant and vegetable leftovers that return their nutrients to the soil as they break down.

Synthetic fertilizer is made in factories and contains the chemicals **nitrogen**, **phosphorous** and **potassium**. Often it is so rich that the plants can't make use of all the nutrients, which escape into the waterways, where they can cause damage.

Why do we need fertilizer?

As they grow, plants take nutrients from the soil, and they become part of the plant. Animals pick the plants and eat them, so they get the goodness of the nutrients—but it means the nutrients are no longer in the soil. So, we need to add more each growing season for the next crop of seeds.

NUTRIENTS

FIBONACCI SEQUENCE

The "Fibonacci sequence" is a sequence of **numbers** that follows a simple pattern. In the sequence each number is made by adding up the two numbers that come before it.

The sequence begins like this:

0 1 1 2 3 5 8 13 21 34 55 89

0+1=1 1+1=2 1+2=3 2+3=5 3+5=8 5+8=13 8+13=21 13+21=34 21+34=55 34+55=89

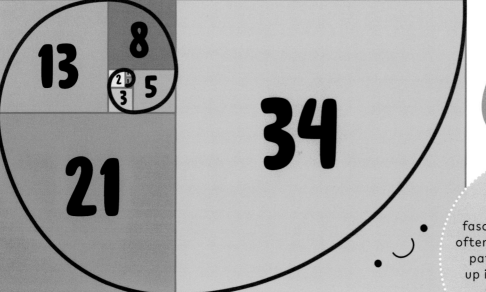

This simple pattern creates an extraordinary effect. If these numbers are used to create squares of that size, the squares fit together neatly into a spiral shape.

That looks nice—but the fascinating thing is how often this mathematically patterned spiral turns up in nature, from snail shells and flower seeds to the structure of the galaxies.

Golden ratio

A ratio is calculated by dividing one value by another. The golden ratio has the value 1.618 and it is "golden" because ratios with this value are seen as particularly beautiful and they are common in nature. Any two neighboring numbers in the Fibonacci sequence have this golden ratio.

35

FIBER OPTICS

Fiber-optic technology allows all kinds of communications—from telephones to TV and the internet—to travel at (almost) the **speed of light**. Light is the fastest thing in the universe so fiber-optic communication is superfast!

Pulses of light travel down fiber-optic cables, which are about the width of a human hair, so they are able to bend.

This small size enables the light to travel so far because of a phenomenon called total internal reflection: when the light hits the side of the cable, it doesn't scatter but bounces off the side at the same **angle**.

The pulses of light bounce, zigzagging, down the cable at the speed of light.

CORE

CLADDING

PROTECTIVE SHEATH

Binary code

Computers translate the pictures and sound into **binary** code, made up of 0s and 1s. This **code** is sent down fiber-optic cables: a pulse of light for every 1 and no light for a 0. At the other end of the cable, another device translates the code and displays it just as it was sent.

FOSSIL

Fossils are the remains of ancient life preserved in rock. Rather than decompose completely, sometimes—very rarely—the conditions are right for a body to become fossilised. There are also trace fossils, which preserve not a body but a behavior, such as a footprint.

Fossilization takes millions of years. When a dead animal is buried in mud, ash, or sand, the soft parts rot away, leaving the skeleton.

To become a fossil, layers of sediment build up (see page 80), eventually turning to rock around the skeleton.

Over time, as water gradually flows through the rock, it dissolves the skeleton, leaving a "mold" in its shape. Over more time, **minerals** from the water fill in the mold, creating the fossil.

Fossil hunting

Although fossils are rare, there are places they are more likely to be found—where rocks are more easily **eroded**, such as the coast or rocky plains.

Many of the first fossils found in England were on the beach at Lyme Regis, and the canyons of Alberta, Canada are home to more dinosaur bones than have been found anywhere.

FRICTION

Friction is a **force** between two objects that are touching one another. The force is invisible but we can sense it at work. When two objects move against each other, friction can make heat and sound and slow down movement.

The less friction there is between two surfaces, the easier it is for them to slide across each other.

Friction depends on the type of material the surface is made from: smoother surfaces create less friction, while the bumpier the surface, the more friction there is.

This is why roller skates and skateboards go so much faster on smooth rinks than on bumpy pavements—and don't work at all on pebbly paths.

Useful friction

On a cold day you might rub your hands together to warm them up. This works because friction between your two hands generates heat (and a little bit of sound if you listen closely). The faster you rub, the warmer they get!

FUNGI

Fungi make up a **kingdom** of living **organisms**. Other kingdoms include plants, animals and insects. Fungi live all over the world—on land, in water, in the air and even inside plants and animals. Scientists think there are around one and a half million different types of fungi.

They are sometimes mistaken as plants but, there are two things that make them different.

First, instead of **cellulose**, fungi cell walls are made from a substance called **chitin**. Also, unlike plants, fungi do not make food from **photosynthesis**.

Fungi come in all sizes. Some are so small you can only see them with a microscope, while at 4 mi², one honey fungus in Oregon, US is the biggest living organism in the world!

Vital fungi

Fungi get their food from the environment, sometimes by decomposing **matter** (such as when they grow on dead wood). If fungi weren't around to decompose them, the world would quickly fill up with dead things! Fungi help return the **nutrients** to the soil and atmosphere, ready to help other living things grow.

10 KM²

39

GEOMETRY

Geometry is a part of maths all about shapes—their **angles**, how they work together, how they can help us, and their special properties.

Geometry is full of facts about shapes. These rules don't change. For example, a square is a four-sided shape with lines the same length, and all four angles are 90° (called a **right angle**).

RIGHT ANGLES

Geometry uses certain tools, such as a **protractor** to measure angles, a **compass** to draw circles and a **set square** to draw right angles.

Three dimensions

Geometry doesn't just look at flat shapes, which are in two dimensions (2D), but 3D shapes too. A 3D version of a circle is a sphere, a 3D square is a cube and a 3D triangle is a pyramid. Looking at buildings you can see how different 2D shapes combine to make new, 3D objects.

GERMINATION

Germination is when a seed starts to sprout and grow on its journey to becoming an adult plant. A seed is **dormant** until it starts to germinate.

To germinate, first the seed must be planted in soil with enough water, and a warm temperature. The seed absorbs water and starts to swell—this is the beginning of germination.

Next, a tiny root starts growing downwards and a shoot starts growing upwards, towards the light.

The root pushes deeper into the soil, sending out side branches to secure the plant in the soil. The shoot grows leaves so it can start making food through **photosynthesis**.

Germination in space

Seeds use **gravity** to work out which direction to send the root (downwards). In space, there is no gravity so seedlings send their roots out in no particular direction. Because astronauts living in space need to help plants grow properly, they guide the shoots out towards a source of light, instead.

GRAVITY

Gravity is a **force** of nature that we see as pulling everything down towards the ground.

Gravity is an **attraction** between all **matter**: the larger the object, the greater the attraction. Things fall to the ground because Earth is the largest object around us, so it attracts other objects with the greatest force.

Earth's gravity also causes the Moon to circle it. The Moon is traveling forwards but Earth's gravity is pulling it towards Earth at the same time. This balance of forces causes the Moon to travel around Earth in **orbit**.

Measuring gravity

Gravity is measured in **newtons**: gravity pulls on an object with the force of 1 newton for every 100 g of its **mass**. This unit is named after **Isaac Newton**, who famously first described gravity when he saw an apple fall from the tree and wondered what made things fall down and not up.

GREENHOUSE GAS

A greenhouse is designed to keep plants warmer than the outside air, and a greenhouse gas is one that sits in Earth's atmosphere and keeps the planet warm, like a thermal jacket. Without greenhouse gases, Earth's average temperature would be around 0°F.

The greenhouse effect works by trapping more of the Sun's energy inside the "greenhouse" than can escape back into space.

In a greenhouse, it is glass that traps the warmth but around our planet it is a layer of particular gases that does the same job.

NATURAL GREENHOUSE EFFECT

HUMAN GREENHOUSE EFFECT

MORE HEAT ESCAPES INTO SPACE

LESS HEAT ESCAPES INTO SPACE

SOLAR RADIATION

GREENHOUSE GAS LAYER

SOLAR RADIATION

The main greenhouse gases are **carbon dioxide**, **water vapor**, and **methane**. Animals produce carbon dioxide through **respiration**, and methane through **digestion**, and water vapor is produced through the **water cycle**.

What's the problem?

Life on Earth depends on warmth so the greenhouse effect is vital. The problem is that over the last 300 years we have been creating so many greenhouse gases that the effect is now so strong, the whole world's climate is changing quicker than nature can keep up.

43

HATCHING

Hatching and cross-hatching are art techniques for adding shade, tone, and texture to an ink or pencil drawing using parallel lines. By adding different tones in different places a 2D drawing can begin to look 3D.

Cross-hatching is another way of building up tone, by placing more layers of parallel lines on top of the hatching, at different **angles**.

Hatching is **shading** in with parallel lines. Playing with spacing varies the tone: the closer together the lines are, the darker the tone looks. The more spaced out they are, the lighter it looks.

To increase the darkness, add more layers of parallel lines, finding a new angle each time.

CROSS-HATCHING

SHADING

STIPPLING

Shading and stippling

Using a pencil, you can change the tone of shadow by how hard you press while shading in.

Stippling uses dots to add different levels of tone: like hatching, the more dots there are, closer together, the darker the area looks.

HYPOTHESIS

All science starts with a hypothesis. It is an idea you might have or a guess about how something works. Scientists need to **test** their hypothesis to see if it is right, or whether it needs to be adapted or needs more research.

When a scientist comes up with a hypothesis, they need to explain their reasoning— why they think what will happen, will happen. They can back up their guesses based on things they know happen in similar conditions.

A hypothesis doesn't have to be correct. The important thing is that it is the starting point for scientific research and testing. The tests should prove or disprove the hyphothesis.

Hypothesis inspiration

Scientists find things to study by observing the world. When they notice something interesting or unusual they come up with a hypothesis for why that thing happens. Most scientists study a small, very detailed part of the world and already know a lot about that area. But anyone can be a scientist by developing a hypothesis and testing it!

45

IGNEOUS

Igneous rock is rock that was once melted and then cooled down. It comes from volcanic lava and makes up nearly all of the Earth's upper crust.

There are more than 700 different types of igneous rock! How quickly the lava cools down shapes the way the mineral **molecules** set, giving each rock its particular character.

Pumice is a lightweight rock that forms when the lava blows out of the volcano and air bubbles form as it falls down and cools.

Obsidian is dark black or green volcanic glass that set very quickly with no mineral crystals. It has sharp edges.

INTRUSIVE IGNEOUS ROCK

MAGMA CHAMBER

Inside or out

Some igneous rocks form outside the volcano, when the lava explodes or flows out of its top, cooling quickly. Not all lava makes it to the surface, though, and some igneous rocks (called **intrusive**) form in chambers underground where they cool slowly.

IMMUNOLOGY

Immunology is the study of our immune system and how our bodies fight diseases. The immune system works all through the body, using **organs**, **tissues**, and lots of different types of **cell** to help keep us from getting ill.

Our immune system can tell apart harmful things that enter the body (called **pathogens**) and things that are useful, such as food, medicine and certain **microbes**.

RED BLOOD CELLS

WHITE BLOOD CELLS

When a pathogen is discovered, **white blood cells** travel in the bloodstream to attack it. B cells fight the pathogen, creating **antibodies**. Each antibody is specially made to recognize the particular **antigen** (a marker) of that pathogen and bind to it.

BLOODSTREAM

ANTIGENS

MARKERS

BINDING SITE

ANTIBODIES

Immunity

We have two types of immunity. **Innate immunity** we are born with and it's a general first response against pathogens. **Adaptive immunity** is more clever because each time the body fights against a new pathogen, it remembers it in a sort of immunity library so the antibodies are ready for another fight. **Vaccines** give us adaptive immunity.

47

INERTIA

Inertia is a law of **physics**. It is **Newton**'s First Law of Motion, and it says that objects stay doing what they are doing unless a **force** acts upon them.

The law of inertia means that a rolling ball will keep on rolling, with the same **speed** and in the same direction.

In reality, we know a ball does not roll for ever. That's because **friction** slows it down, until it eventually stops. On a smooth surface with little friction, like a bowling lane, a smooth ball will roll for longer than a football along bumpy grass.

Inertia also means that objects don't start moving by themselves: they remain still unless a force causes them to move.

Delayed movement

When you're traveling on a train it feels like when it starts moving, you jerk backwards. This is because inertia keeps both the train and your body still. When the force moves the train forwards, it takes a moment for that force to act on your body too.

INSULATOR

Insulators are things that stop **energy** from transferring or "leaking" out to where it's not wanted. This could be heat, sound or electrical energy. The opposite of an insulator is a **conductor**.

Insulators are important parts of electrical equipment because they keep the electricity inside wires, so they can be handled safely.

This works with heat too: in winter a hat insulates your head. Insulation around pipes is called lagging and it helps heating systems work more efficiently, so heat is only transferred from the radiators.

Sound insulation in homes is important to stop your noises leaking into neighbors' homes and annoying them!

Materials

Different materials have different insulating properties. Metal is an excellent conductor of electricity as well as heat and sound: electrical wires are made of copper, and hot drinks quickly go cold in metal cups. Plastic is a great insulator—it is used to coat metal wires and keep hot drinks warm.

49

ITALIC

Type is displayed in three main ways: roman, bold, and italic.

Roman is straight and used for "normal" text—like this.

Bold type is thicker and used for headings and emphasis.

Italic type is forward sloping like this and is used for emphasis.

In writing, italics helps the writer express a deeper level of meaning. Italics means the word should be spoken with more emphasis—and in this sentence, changing the emphasis changes the *meaning* of the sentence.

I'm not doing *that* again.

I'm not doing that again.

I'm not doing that *again*.

Bold text also emphasises words but because they draw the eye in a way italics doesn't, bold is best used for words a reader might search for in text.

Italian type

Both roman and italic text are named for the places they were developed: in **Renaissance** Italy. A Venetian press owner invented italics partly to look like handwriting and partly because with each letter being smaller, more text could fit on a page—so books could be smaller.

Express your ideas in writing
←- - - - - - - - - - - - - - - - - - - →
←- - - - - - - - - - - - - - - - - - - →
Express your ideas in writing

JUPITER

Jupiter is the biggest planet in our **solar system**, and the fifth planet from the Sun. Earth is the third planet from the Sun, so it is colder on Jupiter than on Earth.

Jupiter is a swirling ball of gas (mostly **hydrogen** and **helium**) so it doesn't have a solid surface. We don't yet know if it is gas all the way through or if it has a solid inner the size of Earth.

One day on Jupiter lasts ten hours but a year takes 11.8 Earth years!

EUROPA
(ONE OF JUPITER'S MOONS)

There are big storms on Jupiter, such as one called the Great Red Spot, which has been going on for hundreds of years!

Solar system

There are eight planets in our solar system—which means these eight planets are all in **orbit** around the Sun. They are all different sizes but in order from the Sun out they are:

MERCURY

EARTH

VENUS

MARS

URANUS

PLUTO
(DWARF PLANET)

SATURN

NEPTUNE

KELVIN

Kelvin is the International Standard (**SI**) way of measuring **temperature**. In different parts of the world, people talk about temperature in different ways, such as Fahrenheit and Celsius, but kelvin is the unit scientists use to measure temperature.

One kelvin is the same as one degree Celsius (also known as **centigrade**), so the scale of measuring in kelvin is the same as Celsius. However, the kelvin scale is 273.15° higher than the Celsius scale. So, 0°C (the temperature at which water freezes) is 273.15° kelvins.

0°K is called **absolute zero** and it's the coldest possible temperature.

The scale is named after Lord Kelvin (1824–1907), the physicist who developed the scale.

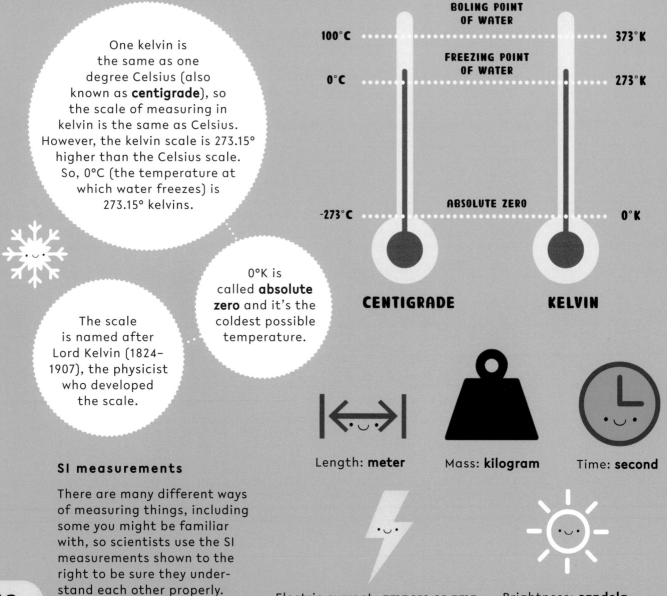

BOILING POINT OF WATER

100°C — 373°K

FREEZING POINT OF WATER

0°C — 273°K

ABSOLUTE ZERO

-273°C — 0°K

CENTIGRADE　　　**KELVIN**

Length: **meter**　　Mass: **kilogram**　　Time: **second**

Electric current: **ampere or amp**　　Brightness: **candela**

SI measurements

There are many different ways of measuring things, including some you might be familiar with, so scientists use the SI measurements shown to the right to be sure they understand each other properly.

KIDNEY

Kidneys are small, bean-shaped organs in your body that remove waste from the blood, which goes on to leave your body as **urine**. There are usually two kidneys working as a pair, sitting in your lower back.

Kidneys filter your blood about forty times a day!

Blood flows through the kidney, squishing through very small vessels and into the one million tiny filters called **nephrons**. Here, water and waste are squeezed out of the blood as urine, leaving the blood clean.

URETER

KIDNEY

BLADDER

URETHRA

ARTERY
(BLOOD GOES IN)

VEIN
(CLEAN BLOOD COMES OUT)

URETER
(CARRIES URINE TO THE BLADDER)

The urine travels out of the kidney through the **ureter** to the **bladder**, where it collects until you go to the bathroom.

Spare kidneys

If for some reason, such as disease, a person has to have a kidney removed, they can live healthily with just one kidney. The remaining kidney grows bigger so it can carry on doing the work that two kidneys did.

53

LIPIDS

Lipids are fats and oils that are essential in the body for it to work properly. **Fats** are solid lipids and **oils** are liquid lipids. They are made of **carbon**, **hydrogen**, and **oxygen atoms**.

We need to eat lipids in our diet to keep our bodies healthy. Oils are found in nuts, seeds, and fish, and fats are in things like butter and cheese.

Inside the body, lipids help make up the cell **membrane**—the "skin" around each **cell**. We also store fat in special fat cells for **energy**. Fat cells under our skin help to **insulate** us against the cold, and are protection for our vital organs.

Mix it up

Lipids do not dissolve in water so if you pour oil into water it won't mix in—unless you **emulsify** them together. This means whisking or shaking the fat, water, and emulsifier together so they stay mixed in small particles. Just like shaking olive oil (a lipid), vinegar, and mustard (an emulsifier) together to make salad dressing!

LODESTONE

A lodestone is a magnet that is naturally occurring (unlike **electromagnets**, which we can turn on and off with electricity). It is found in the ground and its **magnetism** is permanent.

Magnets attract other magnetic materials. This happens because the lodestone creates a magnetic field. A magnetic field has a north pole and a south pole, like this (although you can't see it!):

A lump of iron might be made up of different parts (called domains) where the magnetic fields point in different directions. These domains would cancel each other out so the lump has no overall magnetic effect.

But, if a lodestone is rubbed along a lump of iron, it will make all the magnetic fields in all the domains point in the same direction, so the whole lump becomes strongly magnetic.

Mutual attraction

Magnets will attract and stick to each other if their opposite poles meet. However, if their same poles are brought together (north to north, for example) they will repel each other and never be able to touch.

LOOP

In computer programming, a loop is a piece of **code** that tells the computer how long to keep doing an action for.

Computers don't get bored or tired, so they keep carrying out the same instruction until they are told to stop (and are turned off!).

Words to control loops might include "until," "while," or "when."

To make a robot run a marathon, the program might say:

UNTIL THE FINISH LINE

KEEP RUNNING

Or at school, an instruction for registration could be:

ANSWER "YES" TO THE TEACHER

WHEN THEY SAY YOUR NAME

Repetition

A coding loop can simply say how many times the instruction should be carried out—such as brush your hair TEN TIMES. Loops simplify coding by not having to input the same piece of code the number of times the action should be done, but controlling it with one simple piece of information.

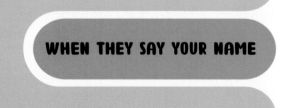

MACHINES

Scientists in the **Renaissance** (about 400–500 years ago) defined a few **simple machines** that use natural **forces** to help do a job more easily. The tools help to make a little bit of work a lot more powerful. These machines are still used all the time in daily life today.

Lever

A lever is made up of a plank and a pivot (called a **fulcrum**). Changing where the fulcrum is positioned, you can lift a heavy thing more easily, or lift a light thing higher.

Wheel and axle

As the small axle turns, the big wheel turns the same number of times, but because it is bigger, it travels further. The axle turns less distance but with more power.

Pulley

A pulley is a flexible rope with a wheel and axle to pull weight in different directions. The more times a rope travels around a pair of pulleys the easier it is to lift weight.

Inclined plane

It's very hard to lift something heavy straight up, but pushing it further up an inclined plane (a ramp) makes the job easier.

Screw

A screw changes a rotating motion into a forwards motion, multiplying the force from the flat end into the sharp, pointy end. It is much easier to twist a screwdriver to push a screw into wood than to push a nail in with our bare hands.

Wedge

A wedge uses its sharp, pointy end to concentrate all the force put on to the wider end into a lot of power at the sharp end.

METAMORPHIC

Metamorphic means to change, and metamorphic rock has changed from **sedimentary** or **igneous** rock by being buried under many layers of sedimentary rock or getting very hot from nearby magma. The rock changes but it doesn't melt.

Rocks become metamorphic deep underground or close to where plates of the Earth's crust meet.

Limestone (a sedimentary rock) becomes **marble** when buried deep under layers that put pressure on it. **Slate** is formed when clay is put under pressure and heat, as if it is being cooked.

It is only by a very long time of the Earth's crust slowly pushing upwards in places, that metamorphic rock makes its way from deep underground to the surface. Eventually, weathering exposes the rocks.

PRESSURE

HEAT

Weathering

Rocks can be damaged by weathering—even hard metamorphic rock like marble and slate. **Acid** can wear them down, which is why acid rain (caused by pollution) gradually wears away buildings. Lemon juice is an acid and can damage expensive marble tops in homes!

METEOROLOGY

Meteorology is the study of the weather. We can all judge the weather by stepping outdoors and using our senses to see if it's wet, dry, windy, or fair. Meteorologists have weather stations with lots of tools to predict the weather.

A **barometer** shows the **air pressure**.

A **hygrometer** measures **humidity** (how much moisture is in the air). The more humidity, the more likely it is to rain.

A **rain gauge** is a measuring cup that catches rain as it falls.

An **anemometer** measures the wind speed by counting the number of times a minute the wind spins the cups around.

A **wind vane** shows the direction the wind is coming from.

N E
W S

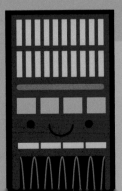

Supercomputers

Meteorologists use supercomputers to look at the **data** they get from weather tools and compare it to models of how the weather has been at similar times. From this, they then predict the weather for the next few days or weeks.

59

MITOCHONDRIA

Mitochondria are an **organelle:** a tiny but important structure inside almost every **cell** of the body. Their job is to help the body make **energy,** so all the other bits of the body can do their jobs too.

CELL

MITOCHONDRION

INNER MEMBRANE

OUTER MEMBRANE

Inside mitochondria are different chemicals: its own type of **DNA**, **nutrients**, and **enzymes.** Reactions in the mitochondria create energy, which is stored in a chemical called **ATP**. The cells use ATP for power.

ATP

Maternal

While almost everything in the body is inherited in combination from a female and a male, mitochondria are inherited solely from the female, with no input from the male.

The more energy each cell type needs the more mitochondria it will have. Liver or muscle cells may even have thousands in each cell! Red blood cells have no mitochondria.

NEWTON

Newtons are the scale we use to measure **force**, with the symbol N. A force is a push or a pull. The greater the force, the greater the measurement in newtons.

PULL OF THE NEWTON METER = 1 N

A newton meter helps us measure force. It is made of a spring attached to a hook, and when the spring stretches with the force, it moves the needle along the scale.

When forces are balanced, an object is still. In this picture, the apple is still so the force pulling the apple down is equal to the force of the meter pulling it up.

WEIGHT OF APPLE = 1 N

Isaac Newton

The newton is named after the English seventeenth-century scientist **Isaac Newton**. He observed the natural world and wrote down some rules about forces that explain why things move, speed up, slow down, or stay still. He discovered **gravity**, which he described as a "pulling force."

NUCLEUS

A **nucleus** is the central or most important part of a place or thing. Almost all animal and plant cells contain a nucleus, as does every **atom**. The plural of nucleus is nuclei—but there's usually only one nucleus in a cell.

In cells, the nucleus is the control center, keeping the work of the cell organized and working as it should.

The most important thing inside the nucleus is **DNA**—the instructions the cell uses to help the body live and grow.

CELL

CYTOPLASM

NUCLEUS

MITOCHONDRION

CELL MEMBRANE

The nucleus is surrounded by its own membrane to keep it separate from the rest of the cell. Inside the nucleus is the **nucleolus**, where **ribosomes** are made. Ribosomes turn information from DNA into **proteins**.

NUCLEUS

MEMBRANE

NUCLEOLUS

NUCLEAR PORE

Channels

The nucleus **membrane** is like a wrapper around the nucleus. Big **molecules** like RNA, ribosomes and proteins can only leave and enter the nucleus through channels called pores. These pores can control what comes and goes.

NUMBER

Numbers are the basic units we count in. Each single number (0 to 9) is called a **digit** and digits combine to make larger numbers. Any whole number is called an **integer**, while part-numbers are called **fractions**.

The order numbers appear – their **place value**— is very important.

When written down, the position a digit is in gives it its value. When the digits 3, 6, 8 combine, the numbers they represent change according to the place each digit is in. 863 is a much larger number than 368 or 683.

This place value system is **decimal**: each place represents ten times more than the place to its right.

DECIMAL PLACE VALUES	100	10	1
NUMBER 863	8	6	3

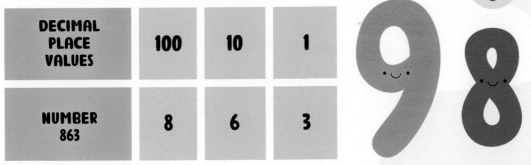

What's in a letter?

Some number values in science are represented as letters. Where the letter is used in an equation, it always represents the same value. For example:

c = **speed of light** = 299,792,458 m/s (meters per second)

NUTRIENT

A **nutrient** is something that is needed to grow healthily—whether for a plant or an animal. Different **organisms** need different nutrients and everything needs a range of nutrients.

Nutrients are needed for **energy**, growth, and repair.

There are three main groups of nutrients: **carbohydrates** (such as potatoes, bread and rice) for energy, **proteins** (including fish, meat and pulses) for growth, and **fats** to keep us warm and protected. We also need to eat **vitamins** and **minerals** in our diet because they do all sorts of important jobs and our bodies can't make them.

Vitamins are vital!

Vitamin A
(in carrots)
helps our eyesight.

Vitamin B
(in meat)
helps us use
carbohydrates.

Vitamin D
(in eggs and fish)
and **calcium**
(in cheese and milk)
help our bones
grow strong.

Vitamin C
(in citrus fruits)
helps us fight
off illness.

Vitamin K
(in green vegetables)
helps our blood to clot.

64

OLFACTORY

The olfactory system gives us the sense of smell. In humans it is one of the five senses, along with **vision**, **hearing**, **touch**, and **taste**. Other animals and plants share these five, and maybe more. Adults can tell apart 10,000 different smells!

NASAL CAVITY

NOSTRIL

What we sense as smells are tiny particles or chemicals that waft into our nose when we breathe in. First, air brushes past tiny hairs in the nasal cavity that filter the air, and a mucus membrane that keeps the nose moist.

SMELL PARTICLES

OLFACTORY MEMBRANE

Why do we need to smell things?

The olfactory system is designed to help us work out what things are safe to eat, and which we shouldn't even touch. When we smell something disgusting, we can't help screwing up our face and moving it away. This helps to keep us safe from germs that could cause us harm.

Then, when the particles reach further back, they dissolve into the olfactory membrane where they are sensed by olfactory receptor **cells**. These send messages along olfactory nerves to the brain—where we process the sense of smell.

ORBIT

An **orbit** is the curved path one thing makes while traveling around another thing. Things travel in orbits at all different scales—from **electrons** in an **atom** orbiting its **nucleus**, to galloping horses on a carousel and even the planets around the **Sun**!

MARCH 21

JANUARY 3

At different speeds and different distances, all the planets in our **solar system** orbit around the Sun.

JUNE 21

EQUINOX

LINE OF SOLSTICE

DECEMBER 21

JULY 3

SEPTEMBER 23

They don't travel in a perfect circle but in an **ellipsis** so sometimes they are closer to the Sun and sometimes further.

Satellites

A satellite is something in orbit around another thing. There are around 30 satellites put into orbit around Earth that make up the GPS system. They constantly beam messages down to the ground that help people find their way around with GPS or satnav trackers.

What keeps them traveling around the Sun is the Sun's huge gravitational pull. Without the Sun and its **gravity**, the planets would fly out in one constant direction.

OZONE

Ozone is a pale blue gas, a form of **oxygen**. It is explosive and poisonous if there's too much of it at ground level, but it forms an important layer in the atmosphere that protects us from the Sun's harmful rays.

The ozone layer is only a few millimeters thick and sits above Earth in the **stratosphere**. It absorbs **ultraviolet** (UV) radiation from the Sun. Without any ozone, the UV would kill off life on Earth's surface. A little too much UV can cause sunburn and even cancer, and also damage your eyes.

OZONE LAYER - - - -

STRATOSPHERE

A hole in the ozone layer developed over Antarctica, making the Sun's rays more dangerous. Chemicals used in aerosols and by industry caused the hole, so countries have limited their use to help protect it.

Ozone molecules

The more common form of oxygen—the kind we breathe in that our body uses—is made up of two oxygen **atoms** bonded together. Its chemical symbol is O_2. Ozone, however, is made up of three oxygen atoms, and its symbol is O_3. It is made when electricity such as lightning passes through the air.

$$O + O + O = O_3$$

67

PERSPECTIVE

Perspective means the way you see something. In art it is a way of drawing so the viewer feels almost like they are part of the scene. Pictures with perspective look more 3D.

The key to a picture with perspective is drawing things smaller the further away they are.

1. Start by drawing the big things at the foreground.

2. Then, mark the **vanishing point** lightly with an X. This is where detail vanishes into the distance.

3. Use a ruler to draw light guidelines from the corners of your foreground object to the X. Now you have a grid to fit the rest of the drawing into.

Proportion

Playing with proportion can also show depth. A person standing straight and still will have certain proportions. But to show that person running towards you, the proportions change: one arm and the opposite leg will be much bigger to show them closer, and the distant foot and hand will be smaller.

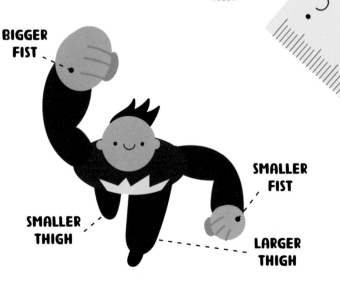

BIGGER FIST

SMALLER FIST

SMALLER THIGH

LARGER THIGH

pH SCALE

The pH scale measures how acidic or alkaline a liquid is. It runs from 0 to 14, where 0 is a very strong **acid** and 14 is a very strong **alkali**. A neutral substance—such as water—measures pH 7.

pH 7

Acids are acidic because they contain hydrogen **ions**, which are very reactive so the more hydrogen ions in the solution, the stronger the acid. Alkalis contain more hydroxide ions, which are also reactive, so the more of them, the stronger the alkali.

Neutral substances contain roughly the same amount of hydrogen ions as hydroxide ions. These two opposite ions balance each other out and make **water**. The further from neutral, the more dangerous the substance is.

pH SCALE

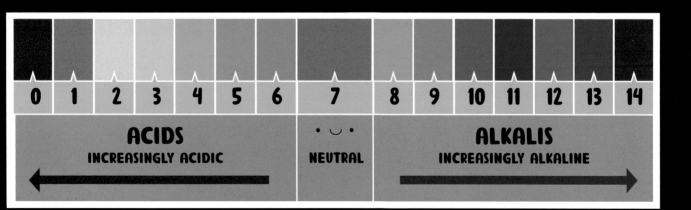

| 0 | 1 | 2 | 3 | 4 | 5 | 6 | 7 | 8 | 9 | 10 | 11 | 12 | 13 | 14 |

ACIDS
INCREASINGLY ACIDIC

NEUTRAL

ALKALIS
INCREASINGLY ALKALINE

Measuring pH

An easy way to measure pH is with litmus paper. It contains a special **reagent** (something that causes a chemical reaction) and when it is dipped into the liquid being tested it turns a color on the pH scale. The pH is revealed by matching the litmus paper with the right color on the pH chart.

69

PHOTOSYNTHESIS

Photosynthesis is the chemical reaction that takes place inside plants to turn sunlight, air, and water into food for the plant.

Photosynthesis takes place in the green leaves of a plant. There, with the power of light, air, and water react to make glucose.

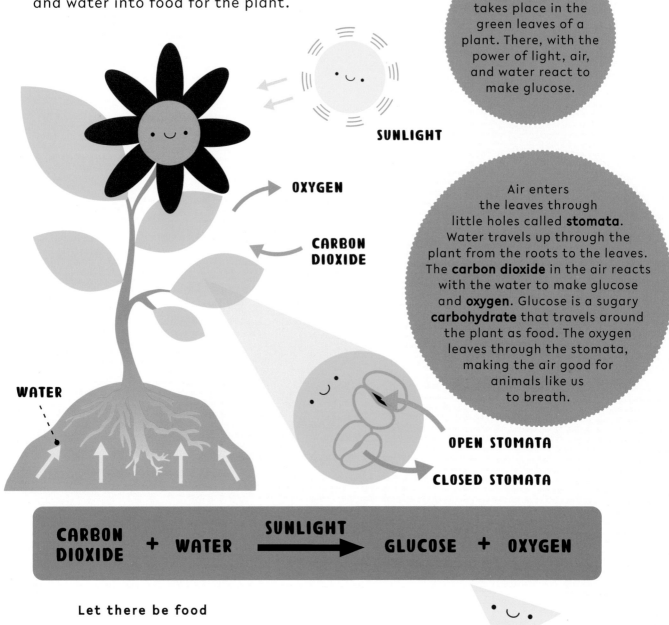

SUNLIGHT

OXYGEN

CARBON DIOXIDE

WATER

Air enters the leaves through little holes called **stomata**. Water travels up through the plant from the roots to the leaves. The **carbon dioxide** in the air reacts with the water to make glucose and **oxygen**. Glucose is a sugary **carbohydrate** that travels around the plant as food. The oxygen leaves through the stomata, making the air good for animals like us to breath.

OPEN STOMATA

CLOSED STOMATA

CARBON DIOXIDE + WATER →(SUNLIGHT) GLUCOSE + OXYGEN

Let there be food

The word photosynthesis means "to put together with light." It comes from the Greek 'photo' meaning 'light', and "synthesis" for "put together." Light provides the **energy** needed to put together the chemicals to create food.

POLYMER

A polymer is a chemical that is made up of many other **molecules** bonded together to make one very large molecule. Often the building block molecules of a polymer are many repeats of the same molecule, repeating in a pattern.

There are both natural and **synthetic** polymers, but they all tend to be solid, moldable, strong and hard wearing.

Plants and animals naturally produce polymers that we make use of, such as wool (made from **keratin** that is also in hair, nails, feathers, and hoofs), silk, rubber, and **cellulose** from wood, used in paper.

Synthetic polymers are plastics. More than 330 million tons are made each year.

One of many

The word "polymer" comes from the Greek for "many parts." A **monomer** is a single part. Polythene is made up of many molecules (monomers) of ethene strung together. PVC (polyvinyl chloride) is made from vinyl chloride combined to make rigid or flexible plastic.

71

PRIME

A **prime** number is special because it can only be divided by the number 1 or by itself. The number 19 is prime: the only way to produce 19 is to multiply 1 and 19 together or divide 19 by 1.

19

FACTORS

1, 19

The number 20 comes after 19 but is not prime as it has several **factors**, for example 2 x 10 or 4 x 5, as well as 1 x 20. These types of number are called composite.

20

FACTORS

1, 2, 4, 5, 10, 20

There are 25 prime numbers between 1 and 100. The number 2 is the only even prime number since all other even numbers can be divided by 2. However, not all odd numbers are prime.

2, 3, 5, 7, 11, 13, 17, 19, 23, 29, 31, 37, 41, 43, 47, 53, 59, 61, 67, 71, 73, 79, 83, 89, 97

2

Prime discoveries

We have been recording discoveries of prime numbers since the fifteenth century. In 1456, the prime number 8,191 was discovered. The longest gap that went between discovering a new prime was 144 years. In 1951 the largest prime ever found without using a computer was discovered, as well as the first prime using a computer.

PRODUCER

In a **food chain**, plants and algae are known as **producers** because they produce their own food. They don't eat anything to get **energy** but create it by turning energy from the Sun into food through **photosynthesis**.

From **bacteria** to plants to animals, all **organisms** need energy from food to live. Different types of organism get their food in three different ways:

Producers turn energy from the Sun into food.

Consumers can't make their own food so they need to eat other plants or animals.

Decomposers such as bacteria and **fungi** get food from breaking down dead plant and animal matter. This helps recycle **matter** so it can be used again.

Food chain

Plants and animals all depend on each other for food. This chain of organisms eating each other is called a food chain. There are lots of different food chains and they combine to make a **food web.** But they usually all start with a plant and end with a **carnivore**.

QUANTUM PHYSICS

Physics is the study of the physical world, and quantum physics is a part that studies **atoms** and particles smaller than atoms (such as **quarks**). Other branches of physics include **relativity**—the workings of the universe as a whole—and **electromagnetism**.

We understand the everyday world we experience and the way it works, but when you look inside the atom, quantum particles act very differently.

For example, quantum particles are always moving about in a fuzzy cloud, and physicists say these particles can exist in all their possible locations at once.

It is only when you look at one of these particles that its position becomes fixed for that moment.

String theory

This is a fairly new part of quantum physics and its scientists are still creating questions rather than answers. The idea of string theory is to combine quantum physics with the things we have already discovered about general relativity, in the hope of providing a theory to explain everything.

QUARK

A **quark** is an **elementary particle**—smaller than an **atom**—that combines with other quarks to make up **protons** and **neutrons** (the particles that make up the **nucleus** of an atom).

The idea of atoms was first formed in the early 1800s: the tiniest particles that made up everything else. "Atom" means 'cannot be cut' so it stands for the smallest particle.

However, scientists later realized an atom is made of even smaller particles: protons, neutrons and **electrons**.

ATOM

ELECTRON

NUCLEUS

PROTON

NEUTRON

QUARK

Later, even smaller particles—quarks— were discovered. We now know there are six 'flavors' of quark: up, down, top, bottom, charm and strange.

Making protons and neutrons

A proton is a combination of two up quarks and one down quark. This balance of quark types gives protons a positive charge.

A neutron is a combination of two down quarks and one up quark. This balances out to give a neutron no overall charge. It is neutral.

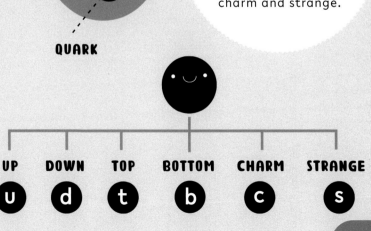

UP	DOWN	TOP	BOTTOM	CHARM	STRANGE
u	d	t	b	c	s

75

RADIATION

Radiation is **energy** that moves from one place to another. Lots of different forms of energy radiate, including **light**, **sound**, **heat**, and **X-rays**. Radiation can happen through a substance, or through empty space.

Energy in the **electromagnetic spectrum** radiates from the Sun. This radiation travels in **waves** through the emptiness of space and reaches Earth.

WAVELENGTH

Radio waves
used in broadcasting

Microwaves
used for cooking, radar, and telephone signals

Infrared
waves for heating

Visible **light**
waves help us see

Ultraviolet
rays tan and burn skin

X-rays
to see bones

Gamma rays
used to kill cancer cells

There are lots of different types of energy in the electromagnetic spectrum and the light we see by is just a small part. The longer the **wavelength**, the further the radiation can travel, but the less energy it has. Short wavelength radiation can't travel as far but has more energy—so can be much more damaging.

Mechanical and nuclear radiation

Not all radiation can travel through empty space. Sound radiates in waves but can only travel through a solid, liquid or gas.

When certain unstable **atoms** break down, they give off **nuclear radiation**. These atoms are **radioactive**, and can be very dangerous as radioactive energy is powerful.

REFLECTION

Reflection is an idea in math, and in physics. Even though they represent different things, they have similar rules and are about a second version of something being reflected from a mirror line.

LIGHT SOURCE

INCOMING LIGHT

REFLECTED LIGHT

MIRROR
(REFLECTIVE
SURFACE)

When you look in the mirror and see your reflection, you're seeing light bouncing off your face and towards the mirror, then reflected back at you.

Light always travels in a straight line. It cannot go around objects but will reflect off smooth, shiny surfaces such as mirrors and polished metal. When light reflects it changes direction by bouncing off at the same **angle** as it hits it.

Mathematical reflection

Reflection in maths is a **transformation**, which means changing a shape. Reflecting a shape happens over a mirror line. Each point of the shape appears the same distance away on the other side of the mirror line. The reflection remains the same size, but "flipped" into the mirror image.

REPRODUCE

When living things **reproduce** they make copies of themselves that will live on after the parent dies. There are two types of reproduction: **sexual reproduction** where two parents create offspring together, and **asexual reproduction**, where the offspring comes from just one parent.

Sexual reproduction is when a male and a female **mate** to combine their **gametes**. Each gamete contains a copy of half the **DNA**, so when the male and female gamete join together the new life contains a complete set of DNA instructions.

Organisms such as **bacteria**, starfish, and some plants reproduce asexually, meaning they just divide themselves into two identical copies.

SEXUAL

ASEXUAL

PARENT

OFFSPRING

MALE

FEMALE

Benefit of sexual reproduction

Needing two parents means sexual reproduction is slower than asexual reproduction, but it has big advantages. Because each individual is made from a unique combination of **genes** from two parents, no two individuals are identical (apart from some twins!). This variety makes a population better at adapting to changes and challenges.

RESPIRATION

Respiration is taking **oxygen** into your body and getting rid of **carbon dioxide**. Breathing is the visible part of respiration but the whole process also involves **gas exchange** deep inside the lungs.

When we breathe in, air passes through the nose and down through the **trachea** to the **lungs**.

The trachea splits into two **bronchi**— one going to each lung. The bronchi split into ever smaller **bronchioles**, which end in tiny air sacs called **alveoli**, where gas exchange happens.

NOSE

MOUTH

TRACHEA

LUNGS

BRONCHI

BRONCHIOLES

DIAPHRAGM

ALVEOLUS

Breathing is controlled by the **diaphragm**, a muscle underneath the lungs. As it contracts, it pulls air into the lungs, and when it expands, it pushes the air back out.

BLOOD VESSEL

CO$_2$ OUT

O$_2$ IN

Gas exchange

Tiny blood vessels sit very close to the alveoli. Here, the gas molecules carbon dioxide (CO$_2$) and oxygen (O$_2$) can move easily between the air and the blood, moving from where there is more of it to where there is less. The O$_2$ moves into the blood and the CO$_2$ moves into the alveoli.

79

SEDIMENTARY

Sedimentary rock is a particular type of rock that is made up by layers and layers of sediment piling up on top of each other and becoming so heavy that over millions of years it turns to rock, such as sandstone or limestone.

The sediment that develops into sedimentary rock is made up of sand, mud, and pebbles. It comes from other rocks that have been worn down by wind and water, and finds its way into rivers and streams.

SEDIMENT

SEA

LAND

LAYERS OF SEDIMENT

As the water flows downhill, it picks up sediment, carries it along, and deposits it further downstream. Most sediment lands in the sea, where it falls to the bottom, gradually building up in layers.

LAYERS TURN INTO ROCK

Sediment

Sediment is the stuff that settles at the bottom of a liquid. You might notice that bits settle at the bottom of a glass of fresh orange juice left for a while. When juice is stirred, the sediment mixes up. The same happens in rivers and streams, which is why water doesn't look clear as it flows along but still lakes and ponds can be clear.

SEISMOLOGY

Seismology is studying the vibrations at the Earth's surface to work out what is happening underneath the surface. This can help find earthquakes, learn about layers of rock, the structure of volcanos and find oil fields.

Seismologists use devices that detect vibrations in the ground. The Earth's crust is made from a few large "plates," which move slowly about, floating on the **mantle** layer.

RICHTER SCALE

GREAT

8.0 OR GREATER
Can totally destroy communities near its epicenter

8

MAJOR

7.0 TO 7.9
Causes serious damage

7

STRONG

6.1 TO 6.9
Major damage to populated areas

6

MODERATE

5.1 TO 6.0
Slight damage to buildings

5

LIGHT

3.0 TO 5.0
Often felt but only causes minor damage

4

MINOR

3

2.9 OR LESS
Usually not felt but can be recorded

2

This movement causes vibrations to travel through the crust. Sometimes the vibrations get stronger, such as when the edges of the plates rub against each other, causing earthquakes or volcano eruptions.

Earthquakes can be mild or severe and are measured on the **Richter scale**.

Tsunamis

If a volcano explodes or an earthquake happens underwater, the vibrations can set off a tsunami wave. Like dropping a rock into a pond, the waves ripple outwards, but as they travel from deep water to shallow near the coast, the waves can reach a huge height. This can be very destructive once the wave hits land.

SEQUENCE

A **sequence** is a series of numbers or other information (such as **DNA molecules**) in a particular order. The order is important as the information held in the sequence has to be understood in that order to be correct.

The Human Genome Project sequenced the entire human genome: the order of DNA molecules (called **bases**) making up each **gene** on each **chromosome**.

We can read the sequence of a person's genome (the list of bases in order) in just a few days—but we don't yet know what each gene does. In some cases, though, we can spot where the sequence has gone wrong and might cause a disease.

The Encyclopedia of Sequences

The Online Encyclopedia of Integer Sequences is a place where mathematical sequences are registered. There are more than 300,000 entries covering all sorts of ideas, from the sequence of **prime** numbers to the sequence of numbers to press on a phone keypad to play the *Star Wars* theme.

SKETCHING

Sketching is an art skill that is useful for quickly getting down an idea, invention, or plan, and a great way to communicate your ideas in a simple way. Sketching also helps you to develop ideas as you draw.

Sketches aren't meant to be perfect—they are just a rough drawing. That's why they are good for helping develop an idea that is still forming in your mind. If the idea is good, you can always improve the sketch. Practicing sketching can help your drawing and thinking, and how you see things.

To sketch an object, first look at what shapes make it up. Start by drawing the biggest shapes, then add in detail.

Top tips for sketching

Try to feel free—draw what you see without worrying about how it looks. Draw big, using as much of the paper as you can—this helps you to feel free and not be too precise. Start off sketching lightly. Then you can rub out any lines you don't like.

SYMBIOSIS

Symbiosis comes from the Greek for "living together." In biology, this term describes two **organisms**, or living things, that are very closely connected. Each of them is called a symbiont.

Honeybees and flowers have a **mutualistic** relationship, which means that they need each other to survive.

Flowers produce **nectar**, which bees use to make their food.

When the bees collect the nectar, the flower's **pollen** attaches to the bees' hairy legs.

The bees take the pollen to the next flower!

Not all symbiotic relationships are so positive. In the case of a **parasitic** relationship, one of the living things benefits and the other is harmed.

Dinner time!

Hermit crabs collect sea anemones and put them on their shells for protection. This relationship is called **commensalism**, from the Latin for "sharing a table." The sea anemone's nasty sting scares away **predators** leaving the crab to hunt for food in peace. In return, the sea anemone happily eats the crab's leftovers!

Fleas gain **nutrients** by biting the skin and sucking blood.

Dogs lose **energy** by scratching until they are sore.

TECTONICS

Tectonics are the way the plates of the Earth's crust move and interact. The land and sea on the Earth's surface are formed of huge rocky "plates" that float on the hot **mantle** layer, rubbing and butting up against each other.

The world's land was once a giant supercontinent called **Pangaea.** About 180 million years ago, Pangaea began to break up into smaller pieces: the tectonic plates, which are still moving now.

MANTLE

INNER CORE

OUTER CORE

CRUST

It is Earth's very hot core that moves the plates. Heat rises so the hot, liquid rocks move up towards the crust where they cool, and then sink back downwards. This creates currents that push the plates apart in some places, and pull them closer in others.

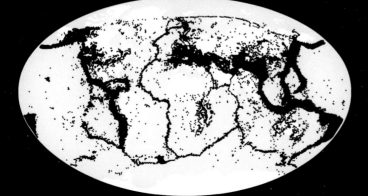

Discovering the plates

Scientists mapped out the borders of the plates by pinpointing the positions of earthquakes and volcanos that had happened. This map—called a plate tectonic model—highlights the border areas of the tectonic plates. **Seismic** activity happens around the edges of the plates.

85

THERMODYNAMICS

Thermodynamics is a part of physics that studies heat and all other types of **energy**, and how they relate to each other. "Therm" means "heat," and "dynamics" is about how it moves between different objects.

Energy is the ability to do work. The first law of thermodynamics says that energy can never be created or destroyed. Energy might look like it has disappeared—such as when a ball rolling across the grass comes to a stop—but the energy simply changes from one state to another.

171°F

57°F

HEAT ENERGY

Heat energy can transfer from something hot to something cold—like how your cold hands warm up when holding a mug of hot drink.

Transfer of energy

Heat, sound, and nuclear energy can be transferred through **radiation**. Electrical energy is transferred from a **battery** to a device by an electrical **circuit**. When an object is high up and able to fall, it has gravitational **potential energy**. When it does fall and start moving, this energy changes to **kinetic energy**.

TRANSISTOR

A transistor is a component used in electronic **circuits** to control how the device works. It can switch the electric current on and off, and help **amplify** the current already flowing. They are used in nearly every electronic device.

Transistors are made of a **semiconductor**— that's a material (such as **silicon**) that conducts electricity in some circumstances but not others. Transistors are controlled by other components in the circuit.

Because the amount of electricity flowing through a transistor can vary, transistors can turn parts of an electronic circuit on and off, or direct more electricity to a different part of the circuit—like directing traffic but for electricity.

Hearing aids

One of the first inventions to make use of transistors were hearing aids. The hearing aid converts sound into electricity, which is amplified (made stronger) when it passes through the transistor. Then the amplified signal is translated back into sound by the speaker—but much louder than it was originally.

TROPHIC

Trophic is a word from **ecology** (the study of **ecosystems**) that is to do with food and nutrition. In the **food chain** of an ecosystem, each **organism** that eats another is at a different trophic level.

The first trophic level in any food chain is the **producer**.

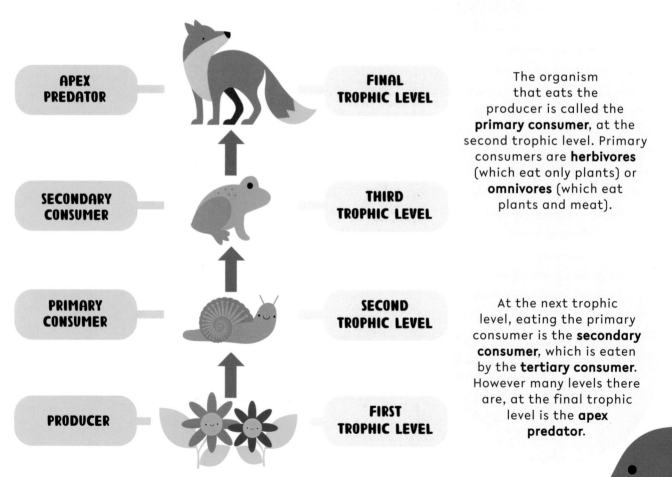

APEX PREDATOR		FINAL TROPHIC LEVEL
SECONDARY CONSUMER		THIRD TROPHIC LEVEL
PRIMARY CONSUMER		SECOND TROPHIC LEVEL
PRODUCER		FIRST TROPHIC LEVEL

The organism that eats the producer is called the **primary consumer**, at the second trophic level. Primary consumers are **herbivores** (which eat only plants) or **omnivores** (which eat plants and meat).

At the next trophic level, eating the primary consumer is the **secondary consumer**, which is eaten by the **tertiary consumer**. However many levels there are, at the final trophic level is the **apex predator**.

Microplastics

Tiny pieces of plastic floating in the waterways are easily ingested by fish as they eat. Because microplastics cannot be digested, when an organism that has ingested microplastics is eaten by a predator, the predator ingests the microplastics too. Once they enter the food chain, microplastics affect every trophic level.

ULTRASOUND

Ultrasound is a technology used to look inside the body without needing to cut it open, and without causing any harm to our insides. The scan can go through the skin or travel into the body on a flexible tube with a light.

Ultrasound scanners use a probe that sends out high-frequency sound **waves** that travel through the **tissues** of the body— the less dense the tissue, the more easily the waves can pass through.

The probe "listens" for the echo of the sound waves as they bounce back from the different tissues inside the body. A computer translates the information from the echoes into an image on a monitor.

Safe viewing

Sound waves are much safer than **X-rays**, so ultrasound is used to look at babies before they are born. The ultrasound can show the baby moving, its heart beating, and can even check how the tiny organs are developing in case the baby will need extra help when it's born.

UNIVERSAL TIME

Coordinated Universal Time (also known as UTC) is the standard way the whole world regulates its time. This helps everyone know what time it is where they are and anywhere else in the world at any moment.

The world is divided up into twenty-four **time zones**, each an hour apart. Even though Helsinki in Finland is on the other end of Earth from Cape Town in South Africa, they are in the same time zone. Some countries change their time in the summer to make the most of the early morning light.

-11 -10 -9 -8 -7 -6 -5 -4 -3 -2 -1

HELSINKI

Each time zone is named for whether it is ahead or behind UTC 0.

CAPE TOWN

UTC 0   +1 +2 +3 +4 +5 +6 +7 +8 +9 +10 +11 +12 +

Spinning Earth

Different parts of the world have day and night at different times, because Earth spins one rotation per day—each day every side of the Earth faces the Sun's light for some time. The time zones are roughly organized so that 1200 midday is when that zone faces the Sun most directly.

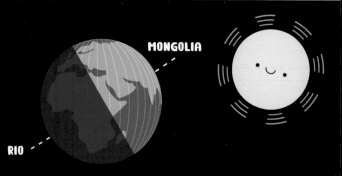

MONGOLIA

RIO

UV

UV is short for **ultraviolet**, which is an invisible part of light on the **electromagnetic spectrum**. Humans can't see it but some animals can.

UV has a short **wavelength**, so it has a lot of **energy** and can be damaging and kill **cells**. On human skin it can cause sunburn, especially on light skin, and in severe cases it can cause skin cancer.

Sunscreen, sunglasses, and clothing are useful protection against UV, and the **ozone** layer protects the planet by absorbing some of it before it reaches Earth.

Protective sunlight

As long as we protect ourselves against damaging UV, it can also help keep us safe. As UV light can damage cells it can also kill germs—so sunlight is a powerful disinfectant. Special UV lights are used in places like laboratories to kill germs and sterilize surfaces.

91

VACUUM

A vacuum is empty space with nothing inside it—not even **air**. Everywhere on Earth is surrounded by air so vacuums don't exist naturally on Earth. Outer space is almost entirely a vacuum.

Although air is invisible, it is full of a mixture of gas **molecules**, dust, **water vapor**, **pollen**, and **microbes**. Air is a miles-thick layer surrounding Earth, and due to **gravity** it presses downwards (**air pressure**). Because vacuums are spaces containing nothing, air will always rush to fill a vacuum.

When astronauts visit space they need to wear pressurised spacesuits containing air and with an **oxygen** supply—otherwise they couldn't survive.

Useful vacuums

We can create vacuums by removing air from an enclosed space. The vacuum then has "sucking" power as air or liquids rush to fill the empty space. Vacuums are very useful for cleaning (sucking up dust) and in pipettes and syringes (to suck up precise amounts of liquid, including medicine).

VARIABLE

A variable is the part of an **experiment** or **test** that can be changed. Designing a good experiment means knowing which part is variable and which parts are **controls**— the things that stay the same in each test.

The best experiments are ones that are designed to test one thing. That thing must be the only variable: everything else must be the same each time.

For example, in a test to see if color affects how high a ball bounces, the color is the variable. Everything else about the balls must be the same: their size, the material they're made from, how high they are dropped from.

Variables in coding

Computers keep track of things that change in a program through variables. It's like a box of information that can change as the program goes on—such as a score in a game. The rest of the program can use the information in the variable to make other decisions.

VELOCITY

Velocity is almost the same thing as **speed**: they are both a measurement of how fast something is traveling. Velocity is how fast something is traveling in a particular direction.

Velocity and speed are measured as the distance travelled divided by the time taken. Cars measure speed in miles per hour (mph) or kilometers per hour (kmph) but scientists usually measure in meters per second (m/s).

I HOUR

Traveling at a steady speed of 60 mph, a car takes one hour to travel 60 miles. In real life, cars rarely travel at a steady speed for the whole journey so the speedometer shows the speed at that particular moment.

60 MILES

Acceleration

Acceleration is when velocity increases over time. It is measured as the change in velocity divided by the time taken to make that change. So, if a person walking at a pace of 1 m/s takes two seconds to increase their speed to walk at 3 m/s, their acceleration is 1 m/s/s (meters per second per second).

VISCOSITY

Viscosity is a way of describing how easily a liquid flows, or how resistant it is to flowing. If a liquid has high viscosity it is resistant to flowing. If it has a low viscosity, it will flow quickly and easily.

Water has a low viscosity. It flows easily—think how water flows from a tap and splashes and spills. Other liquids with low viscosity are oil, milk, and blood. These are all thicker than water to different levels: in other words, they have low viscosity but are more viscous than water.

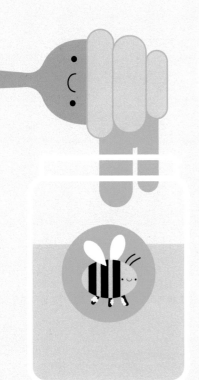

Highly viscous liquids include glue and honey—they are thick to stir and drip slowly.

Temperature

One thing that can change a fluid's viscosity is temperature. If you warm up a thick, sticky honey it becomes less viscous and easier to spread. If you cool down a liquid it can get more viscous.

Car engine oil has a low viscosity even at low temperatures, which allows it to keep the engine running in a cold climate.

95

VISION

Vision is one of our five senses. It uses our eyes to see, and our **optical nerves** and **visual cortex** to process and understand what we are seeing.

Light reflects off objects and travels into the eye through a hole in the front called the **pupil**. The **lens** focuses the light so that it lands sharply on the **retina** at the back of the eye.

PUPIL

LENS

OPTIC NERVE

VISUAL CORTEX - - - - - - - - ➤

IRIS

RETINA

The retina is covered in light-sensitive **cells**—humans have over a hundred million in each eye! These send messages along optical nerves to the visual cortex of the brain, where we process what we see.

Manipulating light

The **iris** (colored part) of the eye opens or closes to control the amount of light entering the eye. In dark places, pupils look huge, and when it's bright, the iris expands to make the pupil opening smaller. Sometimes our lenses don't work properly, so we wear glasses or contact lenses to help.

VOLTAGE

Voltage is the amount of power in an electronic **circuit**. It is the power produced or used, and it is measured as volts (V). The power is produced by **batteries** and used up by components like motors and lightbulbs.

C
(1.5 VOLTS)

AA
(1.5 VOLTS)

AAA
(1.5 VOLTS)

Larger 1.5 V batteries deliver the same amount of power as smaller 1.5 V batteries but for a longer period of time.

In an electronic circuit, the power comes from a source—batteries or the mains electrical supply. The bigger the voltage a battery provides, the more **energy** the components can use.

If a circuit is powered by one 1.5 V battery it would make a motor turn at a certain rate. If you add a second 1.5 V battery to the circuit, the voltage would increase to 3 V, and the motor would turn more quickly.

9-VOLT

AAAA
(1.5 VOLTS)

A23
(12 VOLTS)

0 0.25 0.5

VOLTS USED

Voltmeter

Voltage is measured by a voltmeter, and it tells how much energy is released from the **electrons** in the circuit: it compares the electrons' energy before the component (like this lightbulb) and after to see how much has been given up while powering the component.

97

WATER CYCLE

The **water cycle** describes how water moves around the world, as a liquid, a solid and a gas, and how its journey cycles so that it ends up back where it began. Along the way, it supports all life on the planet.

When there is enough **water vapor** in a cloud, the water falls as **precipitation** (such as rain, hail, sleet or snow).

Warmed by the Sun, water **evaporates**, turning into a gas called water vapor. As the water vapor rises, it cools and **condenses** into clouds.

Back on land, the water, called run-off, travels downhill into streams, rivers, and lakes, eventually making its way back to the sea—where the cycle continues.

The importance of water

More than two-thirds of the Earth's surface is covered in water! As well as being vital for life on Earth, it helps to shape the physical world. As it travels in the water cycle, it slowly erodes rocks and shapes the earth into valleys, creating islands and altering the coastline.

WAVES

Many things travel in **waves**, from sound and light to radio and water. Waves undulate up and down in one direction 90 degrees (**right angle**) from the direction the wave is traveling.

Imagine dropping a pebble into a pond and seeing the waves ripple out. The waves travel out horizontally, while undulating up and down.

WAVELENGTH

AMPLITUDE

AMOUNT OF TIME

FREQUENCY

The height each wave reaches is called the **amplitude** and the gap between the top of each wave is called the **wavelength**. The number of waves in a certain time is called the **frequency**.

Waves keep traveling outwards, gradually losing **energy**, until they stop. If they meet an obstacle they bounce backwards, called **reflection**.

Noise canceling

When waves from two different sources meet, they add or cancel each other out. If they meet in step, they combine to make a bigger amplitude. If they meet out of step, they cancel each other out. This is how noise-canceling headphones work, by canceling out sound waves you don't want to hear.

99

WI-FI

Wi-Fi is the way computers and other devices can connect wirelessly to the internet. The devices communicate using **radio waves**, which work well over short distances. To communicate over longer distances needs cables.

Computers understand information in **binary** code, which can be sent between devices in three ways: as pulses of light in **fiber-optic** cables, as electric pulses in copper wires, or as pulses of radio waves. Radio waves travel invisibly through the air, detectable only by a receiving device, which converts the pulses back into information we can understand.

Wi-Fi connection only works over short distances but a Wi-Fi router connects to the rest of the internet by wires.

Hedy Lamarr

The idea for Wi-Fi technology was developed during the Second World War—by Hollywood superstar Hedy Lamarr. She heard that the US Navy's torpedos, which were controlled by radio waves, kept being sent off-course by the enemy. She had the idea of radio waves "hopping" frequencies to avoid being intercepted.

X-RAY

Discovered in 1895, **X-rays** are an invisible part of the **electromagnetic spectrum** that we use to take photographs of bones inside our bodies. They were named "X-rays" because the scientist who discovered them didn't know what they were!

X-rays can pass through the soft parts of our body but not the dense bone. So when X-rays are fired at a hand placed in front of photographic paper, the bones will block the X-rays and stop them from turning the paper black. The rest of the paper turns black, leaving an image of the bones in white.

The images can show doctors whether your bones are broken, how your teeth are growing, or find certain diseases.

Dangerous rays

At first people didn't realize X-rays were dangerous but frequent exposure to X-rays can cause burns and hair loss, cancer and even death. Today, X-rays are still used in hospitals to look at broken bones and check for organ disease, but they are much weaker and many safety precautions are used.

YANGCHUANOSAURUS

Yangchuanosaurus is a **therapod** dinosaur named after the Yongchuan area of China where it was found. It lived in the Late Jurassic period, about 160 million years ago. It was smaller and lighter than tyrannosaurus rex, with longer arms.

Yangchuanosaurus was about 10 m long and was a **carnivore**. It most likely preyed on other dinosaurs and was an **apex predator**.

Its sharp teeth were curved like daggers to hold on to its prey.

Its eyes faced forwards, so it could judge distances well.

Its long tail helped it balance when running.

SAURISCHIAN

ORNITHISCHIAN

Bird hips and lizard hips

There are two main groups of dinosaurs: those with "bird hips," called **ornithischian**, and those with "lizard hips," called **saurischian**. Therapods like yangchuanosaurus were saurischians, and stegosaurus was an ornithischian. Ornithischian dinosaurs were **herbivores** but some saurischians were carnivores while others were herbivores.

102

YEAST

Yeast is a **microbe**—a microscopically small living **organism**. It is a type of **fungus** that is only a single **cell**, and it is used in kitchens to make fermented food and drink such as alcohol and bread.

Yeast turns **sugar** into **alcohol** and **carbon dioxide** (CO_2). This is called alcoholic **fermentation**. One yeast cell can reproduce itself rapidly to make a whole army of yeast cells, all producing CO_2.

When making beer, the yeast eats sugar in the mixture and turns the beer alcoholic and fizzy, from the bubbles of CO_2.

Making bread, yeast turns sugar into CO_2 gas that gives bread its bubbles and makes it rise. The alcohol burns off in the oven.

Best conditions

For yeast to grow and ferment as efficiently as possible when making beer, certain conditions need to be perfect: the temperature, plenty of **oxygen**, enough sugar and no other damaging microbes getting in the way.

YOLK

The yolk is the yellow part of an egg. It helps to supply food to the **embryo** growing inside the egg. People and animals eat unfertilized eggs because the yolk is very nutritious, containing vitamins, minerals, fats, and protein.

Eggs are laid by birds, fish, insects and reptiles. While the embryo (unhatched baby animal) develops inside the egg it needs food to help it grow. The yolk is the only source of food it has until it has grown enough to hatch.

If the egg isn't fertilized before it is laid, it won't grow an embryo. The egg's contents—the yolk and white—provide food for other animals.

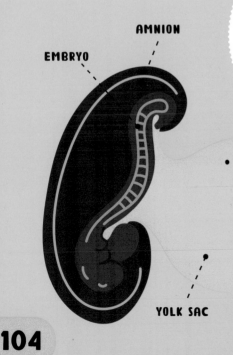

AMNION

EMBRYO

YOLK SAC

Human yolk sac

When a sperm unfertilizes an egg, the **cells** divide and grow into an embryo, which in time develops into a baby. When it is three days old, the embryo develops a yolk sac, which helps supply it with blood. By four weeks, the yolk sac disappears as the **placenta** takes over feeding the embryo.

YTTERBIUM

Ytterbium is a chemical **element**. It is soft and has a bright silvery shine. Its chemical symbol is Yb and its **atomic number** is 70, which means it has seventy **protons** in the **nucleus** of each **atom**.

YB
70

Ytterbium is one of a group of seventeen elements called **rare earth elements** (REEs). They aren't especially rare but they are spread evenly across Earth, so there's never very much in any one place. Ytterbium is mostly mined in China, USA, Brazil, and India.

Ytterbium is used to make **infrared** lasers (a narrow beam of light) and used in small quantities as part of the mixture to make stainless steel.

A quarry-full

Ytterbium is named after Ytterby, a village in Sweden. From one quarry near the village, eight new elements were discovered. From the 1790s, chemists analyzed a black material found there, uncovering new elements that were named for the area: yttrium, erbium, terbium, and ytterbium, which was described in 1878.

YTTERBY

105

ZERO

Zero is the number word for "nothing," or "no value."
If you take away a number from itself, the result is zero.
It took a long time for people to name zero because
it's hard to name something that isn't there.

Before the idea
of "nothing" as a value
was invented (see below),
the Babylonians had come up
with a way to represent it as—

2,300 years ago.

It didn't appear
as a number but the
symbol was used to show
its place in written large
numbers—such as 3,063.
If the zero wasn't there,
the number would be 363—totally different
than 3,063.

The Romans
didn't use zero:
their notation used
single characters for
multiples of ten.

10 = X	100 = C
20 = XX	500 = D
50 = L	1000 = M

Invention of zero

People were adding things together long before we had the idea of
'zero'. In the seventh century an Indian astronomer, Brahmagupta,
invented the idea of 'zero', naming it 'shunya', meaning 'empty'.

In the ninth century, a Baghdad mathematician adapted shunya
into a dot symbol—which developed into the 0 we use today.

ZOOLOGY

Zoology is the part of biology that studies animals and animal life. The animal kingdom is divided into two main groups: **vertebrates** (animals with a backbone) and **invertebrates** (animals without a backbone) and zoology studies them all.

By studying different **species** of animal—how their bodies are formed and how they work, and how they are similar and different from each other—zoologists **classify** species into different groups to show how they are related.

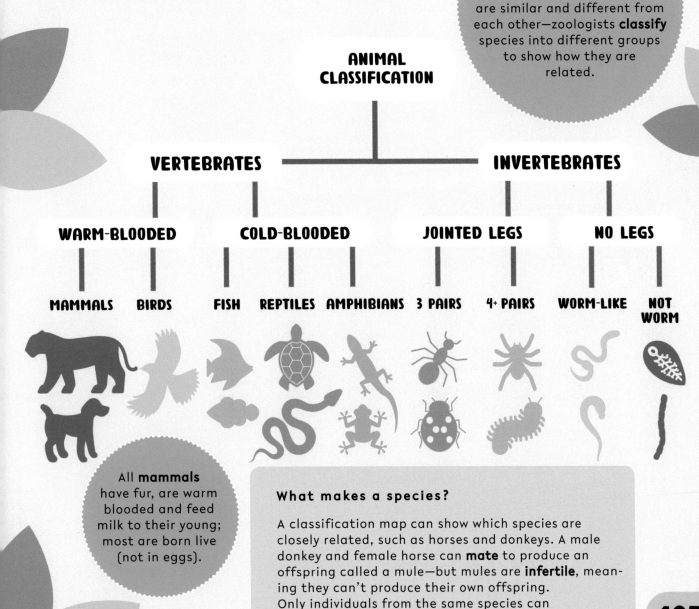

ANIMAL CLASSIFICATION

VERTEBRATES

INVERTEBRATES

WARM-BLOODED

COLD-BLOODED

JOINTED LEGS

NO LEGS

MAMMALS   BIRDS   FISH   REPTILES   AMPHIBIANS   3 PAIRS   4+ PAIRS   WORM-LIKE   NOT WORM

All **mammals** have fur, are warm blooded and feed milk to their young; most are born live (not in eggs).

What makes a species?

A classification map can show which species are closely related, such as horses and donkeys. A male donkey and female horse can **mate** to produce an offspring called a mule—but mules are **infertile**, meaning they can't produce their own offspring. Only individuals from the same species can reproduce **fertile** offspring.

107

INDEX/GLOSSARY OF TERMS

quickly **46**

Oil – lipid in liquid form **54**, **95**

Omnivore – an organism that eats both plants and meat **88**

Optic nerve – the nerve that takes messages to the brain from the eye **96**

Orbit – page 66 for main definition **42**, **51**

Organ – a structure in the body with a specific job to do, such as the lungs or kidneys **47**, **53**, **54**, **79**, **101**

Organelle – a structure inside a cell that has a particular job to do, such as mitochondria **60**

Organic – a substance made from natural things, something that once lived, or contains the element carbon **34**

Organism – a living plant, animal or fungus **31**, **39**, **64**, **73**, **78**, **84**, **88**, **103**

Ornithischia – a group of dinosaurs with 'bird-hips' **102**

Output – the result of a computer program or algorithm **10**

Oxygen – a chemical element usually found as a gas that animals breathe in and plants produce **54**, **67**, **70**, **79**, **92**, **103**

O₂ – the chemical symbol for oxygen **67**, **79**

Ozone – page 67 for main definition **91**

P

Palaeontologist – a scientist who studies fossils **23**

Pangaea – early in Earth's history, all the landmass was stuck together in one big supercontinent called Pangaea **85**

Parasitic – an organism that lives on another organism and causes it harm **84**

Pathogen – a microbe that causes harm **47**

Pedesis – another word for Brownian motion **17**

Phosphorous – a chemical element used in fertilizer **34**

Photoreceptor – a chemical that traps light **19**

Photosynthesis – page 70 for main definition **19**, **39**, **41**, **73**

Physics – the study of the physical world, from particles smaller than an atom to the whole universe **21**, **28**, **48**, **74**, **77**, **86**

Place value – the position a digit comes in any larger number **63**, **106**

Placenta – in mammals, an organ that helps provide nutrients from the mother to the growing baby **104**

Plankton – tiny creatures that live in the sea **16**

Plastic – a synthetic polymer that is very durable and never fully breaks down in nature **49**, **71**, **88**

Pluto – a dwarf planet in our solar system **51**

Pollen – a powdery substance made by flowers that makes their gametes **17**, **84**, **92**

Potassium – a chemical element used in

fertilizer **34**

Potential energy – energy that is stored and ready to be used in a different form **86**

Precipitation – weather that falls from the sky, such as rain, hail and snow **98**

Predator – an animal that preys on (hunts) other animals to eat **8**, **84**, **88**, **102**

Primary consumer – in a food chain, the organism that eats the producer **88**

Prime – page 72 for main definition **82**

Process – the main action part of an algorithm, or a series of actions that have a particular outcome **10**, **19**, **22**, **65**, **79**, **96**

Producer – page 73 for main definition **88**

Program – a set of code that a computer uses to do a particular job **10**, **56**, **93**

Proportion – a way of drawing to show which things are in the foreground (front) and which are further back **68**

Protein – large molecules made in cells that do various important jobs in the body: they are the building blocks of certain tissues in the body such as hair and nails, they fight disease and they help other reactions take place **20**, **62**, **64**, **104**

Proton – a particle in the nucleus of an atom that has a positive charge **13**, **75**, **105**

Protractor – a semi-circle shaped tool used in geometry to measure angles **40**

Pulley – a simple machine to make lifting heavy loads more easy **57**

Pumice – a lightweight rock that forms when air bubbles form inside volcanic lava as it cools **46**

Pupil – the opening in the eye where light is let in **96**

Q

Quark – page 75 for main definition **15**, **74**

R

Radiation – page 76 for main definition **43**, **67**, **86**, **91**

Radio waves – long-wave energy that we use to broadcast sound information via the radio **76**, **99**, **100**

Radioactive – particles that give off nuclear radiation as they break down **76**

Rain gauge – a cup that measures rainfall **59**

Rare earth element – one of a group of chemical elements that are spread fairly evenly across the Earth's surface so there's never lots in any one place **105**

Reagent – a substance that causes a chemical reaction between other substances **69**

Reflection – page 77 for main definition **36**, **99**

Relativity – a part of physics that tries to explain how the whole universe works **74**

Renaissance – a period 400–500 years ago in Europe when people made great developments in science, art and literature **50**, **57**

Reproduce – page 78 for main definition **27**, **103**, **107**

Respiration – page 79 for main definition **43**

Retina – the back wall of the eye that senses light and turns the information into messages to the brain along the optic nerve **96**

Ribosome – the organelle inside cells that turns genetic code into a protein **20**, **62**

Richter scale – a scale to measure the strength of earthquakes **81**

Right angle – where two lines meet at 90° **40**, **99**

RNA – stands for ribonucleic acid, helps cells to turn DNA code into proteins **62**

Roman – text written straight and used for 'normal' text **50**

S

Satellite – something that orbits a planet or star. Can be made by humans or natural **66**

Saturn – the sixth planet from the Sun in our solar system **51**

Saurischia – a group of dinosaurs with 'lizard-hips' **102**

Screw – a simple machine that works by twisting **57**

Second – the standard scale for measuring time **15**, **52**, **63**, **94**

Secondary consumer – in a food chain, an organism that eats the primary consumer **88**

Sedimentary – page 80 for main definition **58**

Seismic – the study of vibrations at the Earth's surface **35**

Semiconductor – a substance that can conduct electricity or not, depending on the situation **87**

Sequence – page 82 for main definition **35**

Set square – a tool used in geometry to draw right angles **40**

Sexual reproduction – when two individuals in a species create offspring together **78**

Shading – a way of changing the tone of a drawing by changing how hard the pencil is pressed on the paper when coloring in **44**

SI measurements – the standard ways scientists measure different things **52**

Silicon – a chemical element used in semiconductors **87**

Simple machines – simple tools that use natural forces to make work easier **57**

Slate – a metamorphic rock formed from